D1709516

The Science of
RENEWABLE
ENERGY

THE SCIENCE OF
BIOMASS
ENERGY

by Cecilia Pinto McCarthy

ReferencePoint

© 2018 ReferencePoint Press, Inc.
Printed in the United States

For more information, contact:
ReferencePoint Press, Inc.
PO Box 27779
San Diego, CA 92198
www.ReferencePointPress.com

Library of Congress Cataloging-in-Publication Data

Names: McCarthy, Cecilia Pinto, author.
Title: The science of biomass energy / by Cecilia Pinto McCarthy.
Description: San Diego, CA : ReferencePoint Press, Inc., [2018] | Includes
    bibliographical references and index.
Identifiers: LCCN 2017042003| ISBN 9781682823019 (hardcover : alk. paper) |
    ISBN 9781682823026 (pdf)
Subjects: LCSH: Biomass energy--Juvenile literature.
Classification: LCC TP339 .M378 2018 | DDC 662/.88--dc23
LC record available at https://lccn.loc.gov/2017042003

IMPORTANT EVENTS IN THE DEVELOPMENT OF
BIOMASS ENERGY

1826
American inventor Samuel Morey designs an internal combustion engine that runs on ethanol mixed with turpentine.

1896
Henry Ford designs the engine of his first automobile, the Quadricycle, to be powered by pure ethanol.

1830s
Wood and grain-based alcohol blends are regularly used as lamp fuels in the United States.

1945
After World War II, lower oil prices hurt sales of ethanol.

1790 **1850** **1890** **1900** **1950**

1796
Johann Tobias Lowitz filters distilled ethanol and obtains pure ethanol.

1900
A French company demonstrates a diesel engine that runs on peanut oil at the Paris Exposition.

1950s
Oil and gasoline overtake alcohols as the most used fuels in the United States.

1862
The US Congress imposes a $2 per gallon excise tax on alcohol that makes ethanol expensive and causes its use to decline.

1930s
While petroleum products become more popular as energy sources, some continue to advocate the use of ethanol as automobile fuel.

2009
The European Union (EU) enacts the Renewable Energy Directive, which calls for the European Union to use renewable energy to fulfill at least 20 percent of its energy needs by 2020.

2007
The Energy Independence and Security Act (EISA) is enacted to increase the supply of renewable alternative fuels.

2014
Scientists at the University of Georgia directly convert biomass to ethanol using genetically engineered bacteria.

1973
The Organization of Petroleum Exporting Countries (OPEC) imposes an embargo against the United States that leads to an oil shortage.

| 1970 | 1990 | 2000 | 2010 | 2020 |

2008
The US Department of Agriculture reveals its National Biofuel Action Plan to cut gasoline consumption and develop biofuel vehicles.

2017
Exxon Mobil and Synthetic Genomics make a breakthrough in biofuel research when they successfully modify a strain of algae to more than double its oil content.

1970
The United States establishes the Clean Air Act, a federal law that allows the government to regulate the emission of pollutants that pose a danger to public health.

POWERED
BY BIOMASS

FROM THEORY TO APPLICATION

The Sun produces enormous amounts of energy that radiates into space. Some hits Earth. Plant leaves can capture this energy. Plants also take in carbon dioxide from the atmosphere and water from the environment. They use the Sun's energy to convert carbon dioxide and water into sugar. Plants change sugar into starch, which is stored in their tissues. When plants are burned, the starches break down into carbon dioxide and water. The stored energy from the Sun is released as heat. Stored plant energy is cycled through animals when they eat plants. Biomass includes all organic matter that comes from plants and animals. People can harness the energy stored in biomass. Biomass can be burned, creating heat. Biomass may also be converted into liquid, gas, or solid fuels. The fuels can be used to generate power in the form of steam or electricity.

About an hour's drive west of Florida's palm tree–lined beaches is a flat, treeless landscape. In an area just south of Lake Okeechobee and north of the Everglades, 67,000 acres (27,000 ha) of sugarcane grow in the swampy soil. The area's fertile earth, warm temperatures, and plentiful water supply make this part of Florida a favorable place to grow sugarcane. It was here that the Okeelanta Sugar Mill and Refinery began growing, harvesting, and processing sugarcane in the 1960s. In 1996, a new facility opened next to the sugar mill. The 140-megawatt (MW) Okeelanta **Cogeneration** Facility (OCF) is operated by the New Hope Power Company. It is the largest woody biomass power plant in the United States. Biomass

facilities use organic waste that might otherwise be dumped in landfills and burn it to generate energy. Inside the OCF, waste materials from the sugar mill, along with wood waste collected from around Florida, are converted into energy. The energy is then returned to the sugar mill in the form of steam power. Excess energy is sold to area utility companies.

Energy from Sugar and Wood

During sugar production, sugarcane is ground up and its juice is extracted. Water in the juice goes through evaporation and is processed into sugar. What's left over is a fibrous material called bagasse. Approximately 30 tons (27 metric t) of bagasse is produced from 100 tons (91 metric t) of compressed sugarcane. Bagasse contains water, which lowers the material's energy content. To reduce the moisture level, bagasse is often mixed with wood chips. Wood chips used at the OCF come from across South Florida. The chips are made from waste wood that comes from clearing land

Sources of biomass are easy to find, as many industries create waste products that can be burned for fuel. Sugarcane bagasse is an example of agricultural waste that can be used for energy.

and tree maintenance. Every year, the OCF converts 800,000 tons (726,000 metric t) of bagasse and 700,000 tons (635,000 metric t) of wood waste into energy.

Professor Martha C. Monroe of the University of Florida in Gainesville writes,

> *Converting two waste products—bagasse and woody debris— into a valuable commodity, power, is an important service the Okeelanta Cogeneration Facility provides South Florida. There are not enough landfill sites to accommodate all the wood waste that the area produces, and burning this wood in open piles would generate far more air pollution. The power plant at*

Okeelanta has been successful at meeting a need for power and doing so in an environmentally friendly way.[1]

When the power plant was installed, a spokesperson for one of the companies behind it noted that replacing the mill's existing energy supply would result in less pollution, saying, "You'll see a substantial reduction in **emissions** from the mill."[2]

The Biomass Industry Today

Cogeneration plants, also called combined heat and power (CHP) plants, like the Okeelanta facility are just one way that biomass is processed into energy. Other burning methods result in solid materials that resemble charcoal or oils that become transportation fuels. Oils can also be processed into biogas. Food crops containing large amounts of sugar are **fermented** to yield alcohols such as ethanol. Processing biomass materials with chemicals is another way to get energy from them.

> **WORDS IN CONTEXT**
>
> **emissions**
> Pollutants discharged into the air.
>
> **fermented**
> Broken down chemically by bacteria, yeasts, or other microorganisms.

Even used cooking oils can be converted into combustible fuels for transportation. Many restaurants are willing to give away their used oils for this purpose. The magazine *Car and Driver* notes, "Restaurants pay to have their used oil hauled away, so it's likely they'll be delighted to have you haul it away for nothing."[3]

Bioenergy is among the world's most widely used renewable energy sources. It supplies 10 percent of the world's energy. Biomass energy is the basic energy source for people in developing countries. People burn wood, plant residues, and animal waste for heating or cooking on open fires. Countries worldwide are turning to biomass as a renewable resource that not only produces energy but also provides a means of dealing with pollution and waste. One of the benefits of biomass is that it is readily available around the planet. Many types of biomass can be harnessed for energy. Trees and wood waste are a primary source of biomass that is burned for heat or electricity. Crops such as corn, sugarcane, and grasses are grown, harvested, and processed into fuels. Household solid waste and animal waste can also be burned to produce heat and electricity. This cuts down on how much waste ends up in landfills. The US Energy Information Administration explains that "burning reduces the volume of waste by about 87%."[4]

Is Biomass the Alternative Energy of the Future?

While biomass is easily sourced and versatile, it can be difficult to produce it in large enough quantities to compete with fossil fuels. Work also needs to be done to ensure that biomass energy is **renewable**, **sustainable**, and cost-effective. Presently, fossil fuels are often needed to grow and harvest biomass sources. Fossil fuels power the facilities where biomass is processed. In some cases, treating biomass requires several steps. The added procedures drive up the cost of production. In some areas, large tracts of land are cleared to grow crops for biomass instead of food. This results in competition between food and fuel crops. Clearing land also causes the destruction of forests. If biomass is to compete with petroleum and other fossil fuels, the biomass industry must overcome these obstacles.

While the future of biomass is still uncertain, the industry is making great strides. Between 2002 and 2013, biomass energy consumption in the United States rose more than 60 percent. During that same period, the conversion of biomass to biofuels grew more than 500 percent. In 2016, US imports of biodiesel and renewable diesel made from biomass reached a record high of 916 million gallons (3.5 billion L). Researchers are working on new technologies to overcome some of biomass energy's limitations. The US Office of Energy Efficiency & Renewable Energy publication *2016 Billion-Ton Report* described a promising future for biomass energy:

> *In summary, results in this report indicate the United States holds great potential for production of biomass feedstocks. In broad terms, a diversity of biomass resources could be tapped that could double or triple current levels of biomass use for bioenergy, producing approximately 1.0–1.5 billion tons [0.9–1.4 billion metric t] of biomass annually for energy and co-products.*[5]

1

HOW DOES BIOMASS ENERGY WORK?

Biomass is made up of organic matter. Organic matter is living and comes from plants and animals. The energy in this matter originates from sunlight. Plants, algae, and some types of bacteria can capture the Sun's energy through a process called photosynthesis. Plants contain pigment molecules, such as green chlorophyll. During photosynthesis, chlorophyll absorbs energy from sunlight. Plants also take in carbon dioxide and water from their surroundings. Through a chemical reaction, the absorbed energy converts carbon dioxide and water into carbohydrates and oxygen. Carbohydrates include sugars, starches, and cellulose. Some of the carbohydrates produced are used by the plant for energy, and some are stored. Plants store them in their leaves, stems, and roots. When a plant is eaten by an animal, the energy in the carbohydrates is transferred to the animal's body. When plants and animals die, microorganisms decompose the remains. Once again, the energy that originally came from the Sun is transferred.

Biomass contains proteins, carbohydrates, and lipids. Lipids are fats and oils. Carbohydrates and lipids are made up of long molecules of carbon, hydrogen, and oxygen. When biomass is burned, the chemical bonds in these molecules are broken and energy is released. Some biomass sources are crops grown specifically as biomass. Others are waste products from other industries. Common crops used in the bioenergy industry include corn, sugarcane, trees, and grasses. Waste can come from the wood industry, household garbage, animal dung, and other sources. Biomass may be used directly or indirectly. When biomass is used directly it is burned. Burning releases chemical energy as heat. When biomass is used indirectly, it is first processed and converted into another form. A variety of methods are used to change biomass into liquid biofuels, biogas, or solid fuels. Biomass energy is a renewable source of energy, because more plants can be grown to replace the ones used.

Fossil fuels also contain energy from the Sun. These fuels are the remains of plants and animals that died millions of years ago. The ancient organisms, along with the energy stored in them, were buried under layers of rock. Underground, the remains were subjected to intense heat and pressure. Eventually, they became coal, oil, or natural gas. They are brought to the surface by mining, drilling, or other processes. When fossil fuels are burned, they release their stored energy. Burning them also creates air pollution, releasing carbon dioxide and other harmful gases. Fossil fuels are not renewable. Using them diminishes the remaining supply. It would take millions of years to make more fossil fuels. As the US Energy

Information Administration explains, "Energy sources are classified as nonrenewable because they do not form or replenish in a short period of time."[6]

The Carbon Cycle

Carbon is the basic building block of all life. Carbon moves through Earth's atmosphere, oceans, land, and rocks in slow and fast cycles. The slow carbon cycle occurs when carbon is stored in rocks, in fossil fuels, and deep in the ocean. It can stay in these places for 100 to 200 million years. This carbon is eventually released by volcanic activity or other processes, including human burning of fossil fuels. The fast carbon cycle occurs as carbon moves through organisms on Earth. During photosynthesis, plants take in carbon dioxide from the environment. When plants are eaten or die, the carbon is transferred to another organism, the soil, or the air. Carbon dioxide in the atmosphere increases during the winter when there is less photosynthesis and some plants die and decompose. When plants grow during the spring and summer, atmospheric carbon dioxide levels decrease.

When biomass is burned, it releases carbon dioxide into the atmosphere. Under ideal conditions, burning biomass is carbon neutral. The amount of carbon dioxide released by burning biomass is offset by the amount of carbon dioxide taken in by living plants. Being carbon neutral is important. If too much carbon builds up in the atmosphere, it traps the Sun's heat, preventing it from reflecting back into space. This can affect global climate.

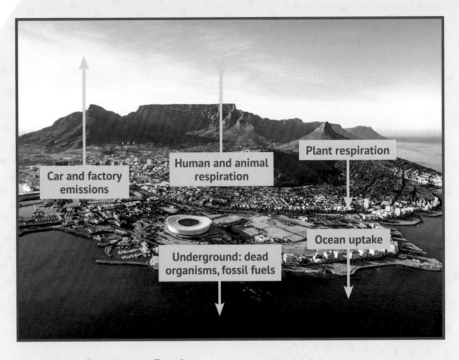

Car and factory emissions

Human and animal respiration

Plant respiration

Ocean uptake

Underground: dead organisms, fossil fuels

The Carbon Cycle

In the carbon cycle, carbon moves through the air, land, and sea in various forms. People and animals give off carbon dioxide in the process of respiration, or breathing. Plants absorb carbon dioxide in the process of photosynthesis, and the ocean takes in carbon dioxide from the atmosphere. Underground, carbon is stored in the tissues of dead and decaying plants and animals. Eventually it becomes fossil fuels. When fossil fuels are extracted and burned in factories, cars, or other places, that stored carbon is released again.

The carbon cycle is critically important. The National Aeronautics and Space Administration (NASA), which studies the atmosphere, says, "Carbon is the backbone of life on Earth. We are made of carbon, we eat carbon, and our civilizations—our economies, our homes, our means of transport—are built on carbon."[7]

Sources of Biomass

Biomass sources are known as feedstocks. There are four main types of feedstocks: crops, agricultural waste, forestry residues, and local landfill and industrial wastes. Crop feedstocks are divided into food crops and energy crops. Food crops are a major source of biomass energy. They include many types of crops also used for food products, such as corn, soybeans, and sugarcane. Energy crops are nonfood plants. Many are grown exclusively for use as biomass feedstock. Poplar and willow trees and several types of grasses are energy crops. The best plant feedstocks provide a high yield of material and require a minimum of land and other resources to produce and process.

Agricultural waste comes from crops grown for food, clothing, or animal feed. Harvesting these creates waste materials, such as husks, that can be burned for energy. Agricultural waste also includes animal manure from farms. Manure can be burned or processed for gas.

Forestry residues make up a large part of feedstock used worldwide. Waste wood from the paper and timber industries, trees cleared during construction, and trees downed because of disease, insects, or fire damage are all valuable energy resources.

Garbage from homes and industries offers a constant supply of biomass. Landfills contain municipal solid waste (MSW), which is made up of household trash. One problem with using garbage is that it often contains toxic materials that need to be removed before the biomass can be processed. New systems and technologies are being developed to efficiently and effectively deal with landfill and industrial wastes.

Biomass into Energy

Biomass is the oldest energy source. Since the discovery of fire, wood and other biomass has been burned to keep people warm and cook their food. Many people around the world still burn wood or animal dung on open fires or stoves. But traditional burning is an inefficient way to harness the energy of biomass. Wood and animal dung have a high percentage of water, so they store and give off little energy. New technologies provide people with better ways to harness biomass energy.

There are three methods for converting biomass into energy: thermal conversion, biochemical conversion, and chemical conversion. These methods break down the chemical bonds in the biomass's molecules, releasing energy. Once biomass is broken down, it can be further processed into different fuels. Thermal conversion is the oldest way to convert biomass to energy. Heat and varying amounts of oxygen convert biomass into solid, gas, or liquid fuel. Biochemical conversion uses fermentation to break down sugars, which are then converted into alcohols. In chemical conversion, the biomass source is oil from animal fats or plants. The extracted oil is mixed with alcohol to produce fuel.

Biofuel from Algae

Algae is a promising source of biofuel. It offers a way to produce large amounts of biomass in just days. Algae are small, plantlike organisms. There are more than 100,000 different strains of algae. They can live in freshwater, salt water, or even wastewater. Algae produce energy through photosynthesis. Certain types of algae store the energy they make as natural oils. The oils can be extracted for use as a biofuel. Several methods are used to break down the algae's cell walls so that oils are released. Algae can be pressed or mixed with solvents. The result is biofuel and glycerol.

One of the benefits of using algae is that it can be easily cultivated. Acres of algae grow in sunny open pond systems called raceways. Paddle wheels circulate the water and algae. Different types of algae have specific growing conditions. These conditions can be controlled by growing algae in closed ponds with artificial light. Closed ponds also keep out other organisms that may interfere with growth. Like plants, algae take in carbon, making their cultivation close to carbon neutral. Scientists are experimenting with different types of algae farmed under differing conditions to develop productive strains. In June 2017, oil company Exxon Mobil and genetics research company Synthetic Genomics announced a scientific breakthrough. Researchers modified a strain of algae to increase its oil content from 20 percent to more than 40 percent. One of the scientists said, "This key milestone in our advanced biofuels program confirms our belief that algae can be incredibly productive as a renewable energy source with a corresponding positive contribution to our environment."

Quoted in "Breakthrough in algae biofuel research reported," *Science X,* June 20, 2017. phys.org.

Methods of Thermal Conversion

Thermal conversion uses heat to change biomass feedstock into energy. There are four types of thermal conversion: combustion, gasification, pyrolysis, and hydrothermal liquefaction (HTL). Combustion, gasification, and pyrolysis use different temperatures, pressures, and amounts of oxygen to break down and convert biomass into a variety of fuels. Biomass that undergoes HTL is subjected to high temperatures and pressures but also uses water to assist in breaking down chemical bonds.

Burning biomass when oxygen is present is called direct combustion. A simple campfire is an example of this. The process is used in power plants, too. Before feedstock such as wood waste is burned, it undergoes a pretreatment process to dry it out. After drying, the feedstock is burned at temperatures between 329°F and 608°F (165°C and 320°C). The low heat breaks down tough, woody plant fibers. The result is a brittle, energy-dense bio-coal. Bio-coal is easy to store and transport, and it has a long shelf life. Bio-coal can be burned to produce heat. It may also be used in a boiler to produce steam. The steam then spins turbines, generating electricity. British energy company executive Dorothy Thompson explains that making electricity from wood isn't too different from burning wood for heat in ancient times, but people still think of it differently: "Burning trees is fairly old. Burning trees for electricity somehow in people's minds seems different."[8]

Gasification takes place when the biomass is heated to extremely high temperatures of 1,200°F to 2,550°F (650°C to 1,400°C) in the presence of a controlled amount of oxygen and steam. The biomass does not burn. Instead, the process produces gases. They include hydrogen, carbon monoxide, and carbon dioxide. When the hydrogen combines with carbon monoxide, it forms synthesis gas, also called syngas. Syngas can be used to generate electricity.

Sometimes biomass is heated without oxygen at temperatures of 800°F to more than 1,470°F (430°C–800°C). This process, pyrolysis, decomposes the biomass into solid and liquid parts. The solid is a type of charcoal called biochar, a solid black carbon material. The liquid result of pyrolysis is bio-oil, a dark brown liquid.

One of the most promising conversion techniques currently being researched is HTL. This process is a type of pyrolysis. While pyrolysis requires starting with dry biomass, HTL can begin with wet biomass. Wet biomass feedstocks include manure or food waste, woody crop residue, and algae. The HTL process is similar to the natural processes involved in the creation of fossil fuels. Biomass under heat and pressure in the presence of water is converted into oil. Under normal conditions, water does not react with the biomass. But under high temperature and pressure, water can decompose biomass. The water breaks chemical bonds. Large biomass molecules are broken into smaller segments that re-form into crude oil. HTL processing has several benefits. First, it can accept a large variety of biomass feedstocks. HTL can begin with wet biomass. All other conversion

Landfills overflow with accumulated trash and other waste that could otherwise be used for energy production. New technologies are being developed to remove toxins from waste and turn waste gasification into standard practice.

techniques must begin by drying feedstock. The extra step adds time and cost to processing. HTL also does not require the use of damaging chemicals to break the molecular bonds. The US Department of Energy notes that HTL "uses water as the medium to heat the biomass, which makes it very clean. There are also no harmful byproducts of this process."[9]

Applications of Thermal Conversion

Thermal conversion methods generate energy for cities and industries. During combustion, biomass is burned at a high temperature to produce steam. The steam is used to run a turbine connected to a generator. The generator produces electricity. There are several feedstocks that can be used, including wood and agricultural waste products such as husks. The most efficient use of direct combustion is cogeneration. In other types of power plants, heat is created and wasted, but in cogeneration the heat can be put to good use.

Biomass can be burned along with a fossil fuel such as coal. This type of combustion is called co-firing. Co-firing reduces the pollutants, such as sulfur, that are released by burning coal alone. It also reduces the cost of generating electricity compared with burning only coal. The Drax power station in the United Kingdom is the world's largest co-firing plant and one of the country's largest producers of energy. Originally, the plant burned only coal. But burning coal releases high amounts of carbon dioxide into the atmosphere. In order to lower carbon emissions, Drax began burning biomass with coal at all six of its power units in 2003. Since then, Drax has gradually converted three of the power units to run exclusively on biomass. By converting to co-firing and biomass-only processes, Drax is reducing harmful emissions. Eventually, Drax plans to eliminate all coal use and rely solely on wood pellets. Andy Koss, an executive at Drax, noted that "Drax is playing a leading role in helping to change the way energy is generated, supplied, and used as the UK moves to a low carbon future. Our biomass generating units deliver carbon savings of 80 percent compared to when they used coal."[10]

Gasification creates energy from wood pellets, wood wastes, and crop residues. The gasification of biomass results in the production of **syngas**. Then the resulting syngas is converted into ethanol and synthetic diesel fuel. Syngas itself can be used to power turbines and create electricity. Since the 1950s, it has also been used in the production processes for chemicals and fertilizers.

Gasification is helping solve the growing global problem of MSW. The World Bank's 2012 report on global solid waste management projected that cities would generate about 2.4 billion tons (2.2 billion metric t) of solid waste by 2025. One type of gasification process, called plasma gasification, may help dispose of MSW. Plasma is a state of matter that forms when an electrical charge passes through a gas. Lightning flashes are an example of plasma. Plasma torches are used to generate extremely high temperatures up to 10,000°F (5,500°C). The extreme heat speeds up the gasification process. During plasma gasification, the heat created by the torches converts the biomass to syngas. Any impurities that remain are melted and fused into materials that can be used for such things as road construction and roofing. Japan currently operates three plasma gasification plants. The first plant in Yoshii was constructed in 1999. The plant processes 24 tons (22 metric t) of MSW per day. Steam produced by gasification is used in industry. Not only does the plasma plant produce energy and prevent MSW from ending up in a landfill, but it also outputs fewer emissions than burning waste at incineration plants.

Using pyrolysis, agricultural wastes such as wood chips and plant residues can be converted into useful fertilizers and fuels. One product of pyrolysis is biochar. Biochar is mainly used in agriculture, where it enriches soil and helps the soil retain water. About 50 percent of the carbon from the biomass feedstock is contained within the biochar. This makes biochar ideal for sequestering carbon, meaning that rather than being released into the atmosphere, the carbon is stored in the biochar. Another pyrolysis product is bio-oil, a type of tar. It can be burned to generate electricity. Bio-oil is often blended with other fuels for use in diesel engines.

Biomass feedstocks such as algae are a challenge to process because they contain large quantities of water. HTL is an ideal conversion technique because it can utilize wet feedstocks that are minimally processed. In fact, HTL is such a flexible method that it uses all types of feedstocks. The resulting bio-oil is especially desirable because it can be used in some engines without extra processing.

Methods of Biochemical Conversion

One type of biochemical conversion is anaerobic digestion. In this biological process, bacteria are used to break down large biomass molecules. The term *anaerobic* means that the process takes place without oxygen present. Manure from livestock is a common biomass for anaerobic digestion. Other biomass sources for this process include waste from food and paper industries, sewage, and MSW.

Anaerobic digestion of biomass involves three steps. First, the biomass is placed in a digester tank with water. The water decomposes the biomass. Long carbohydrate molecules are broken down into smaller sugar molecules. Second, bacteria are added to the mix and fermentation begins. The bacteria change the sugars into acids. In the final step, methane-creating bacteria called methanogens convert the acids into high-energy biogas. Biogas is composed of methane and carbon dioxide. Methane can be burned as fuel and used to generate electricity.

Another type of biochemical conversion makes biofuels by first fermenting the biomass. One of the most commonly produced biofuels is ethanol, a type of alcohol. It is often blended with gasoline and used as transportation fuel. Ethanol is known as a first-generation biofuel because it is made directly from a food crop. It is produced from starchy or sugary feedstocks such as corn, wheat, sorghum, or sugarcane. In the United States, ethanol is made from a mix of 90 percent corn and a 10 percent mix of wheat and sorghum. To make ethanol, corn is put through a multistage fermentation process. First, ground corn is mixed with water. Then the mixture is heated and **enzymes** are added. As the mixture cooks, the heat and enzymes break down the starch and convert it into sugar. Yeasts are added and fermentation begins. During fermentation, the yeasts break down the sugar into carbon dioxide and ethanol. Once fermentation is complete, the mixture is reheated. This step is called distillation. The ethanol evaporates

WORDS IN CONTEXT

enzymes
Substances found in living organisms that help cause chemical reactions.

Many commercial livestock farms are installing biogas processors. This investment allows them to efficiently use agricultural waste, such as manure, to generate power.

and the vapor is collected. Finally, the ethanol vapor is cooled and condensed. After water is removed from the liquid ethanol, the ethanol can be blended with gasoline for use in cars and trucks. The use of biofuel blends reduces the emissions of carbon and pollutants.

Analysis of greenhouse gas emission reductions in 2015 due to ethanol show a decrease of 45.4 million tons (41.2 million metric t). This is the equivalent of eliminating 8.7 million cars from roads for a year.

According to a report published by the Renewable Fuels Association (RFA) in 2016, "ethanol biorefineries in 29 states produced a record 14.7 billion gallons [55.6 billion L] of high-octane renewable fuel" in 2015.[11] The leftover solids from the fermentation process do not go to waste. They are dried and fed to livestock. The RFA also noted that the resulting solids were used to create "[44 million short tons] 40 million metric tons of high-protein animal feed."[12]

Applications of Biochemical Conversion

Biogas plants may be large in scale and used at industrial sites such as wastewater treatment plants. Smaller anaerobic digesters can be placed onsite at farms. Digester systems use a variety of bacteria to effectively process waste at different temperatures. Anaerobic digestion is used to decompose agricultural, municipal, and industrial wastes. Food waste, animal manure, wastewater sludges, and sewage are converted into biogas. When processed, biogas can be used as a transportation fuel. It is also used to generate electricity and heat. Producing biogas eliminates pollution and sequesters carbon, too.

According to the US Department of Energy, there were more than 200 anaerobic digester systems operating on commercial livestock farms in the United States in 2015. Dennis Brubaker installed an anaerobic digester on his swine farm in 2011. He chose a digester to help control energy costs. The digester allowed the farm to generate 2.5 times its electric needs and offset half of its heating costs. When asked about the biggest benefits of operating the digester, Brubaker noted, "We found a way to dispose of 7 million gallons [26.5 million L] of manure annually and achieve a tremendous cost savings. We added revenue to the farm through energy savings and sale of excess electricity, and are also able to use the waste heat to heat our nursery barn."[13]

Food crops are most commonly used to produce ethanol. Corn is the preferred ethanol feedstock used in the United States. In Brazil, it is made from sugarcane. The United States and Brazil are the top ethanol-producing countries in the world. In the United States, ethanol production increased from 3.4 billion gallons (12.9 billion L) to 14.3 billion gallons (54.1 billion L) between 2004 and 2014. This large increase in ethanol production was the result of legislation requiring more biofuel to be blended with gasoline. Blended fuels are labeled according to the percentage of ethanol and alcohol they contain. E10 is 10 percent ethanol and 90 percent gasoline. The Department of Energy calculates that "more than 97% of US gasoline contains ethanol."[14] Much of this comes as E10. The largest ethanol plant in the United States is located in Decatur, Illinois. This ethanol is sent to large energy company refiners, where it is blended into gasoline. By-products left over after ethanol is produced are converted into animal feed.

Methods of Chemical Conversion

Chemical reactions break down biomass to convert it into renewable fuels such as biodiesel. Biodiesel is made from oils and animal fats. Oils come from crops such as palm, soybeans, or rapeseed. Used cooking oil may also be recycled to make biodiesel. Biodiesel is created using a process called transesterification. Fats and oils are made up of compounds called esters. During transesterification, alcohols are added to the fat or oil. This leads to a chemical reaction that separates the oil into the biodiesel fuel and a liquid called glycerol. Glycerol is an ingredient used in cosmetics, medicines, and many other products. The biodiesel can be used alone as fuel, or it can be blended with petroleum. Biodiesel has lower emissions than petroleum diesel.

CAN BIOMASS ENERGY
REPLACE FOSSIL FUELS?

F ossil fuels include coal, oil, and natural gas. They are found in Earth's crust. These substances are made from the remains of plants and animals that lived millions of years ago. When the plants and animals died, they were buried under layers of sediment and rock. Different combinations of organisms, along with varying temperatures and pressures, determined what type of fossil fuel formed. Fossil fuels are the most-used sources of fuel worldwide, with oil in the lead.

In 2015, fossil fuels accounted for 78.4 percent of global energy consumption. Bioenergy provided an estimated 10.5 percent of global energy consumption. In the energy race, fossil fuels are still at the head of the pack. But in the future, will it be possible for biomass energy to take the lead? Weighing the pros and cons of fossil fuels and biomass energy provides some insight in answering this question.

Coal formed from organic matter buried in swamps and peat bogs. This hard, black material is high in energy. Coal is extracted from areas near Earth's surface or from deep underground reserves. In the late 1700s, Scottish inventor James Watt patented the steam engine. The engine used burning coal to power its moving parts. Soon industries everywhere were using coal-fueled steam engines. In power plants, coal is burned in furnaces to create steam. The steam spins a turbine shaft to create electricity. In 2016, the US Energy Information Administration noted, "Coal was the source of about 30% of the electricity generated in the United States."[15]

Oil is found as a liquid in underground reservoirs around the world. It is also found in a type of rock called shale. Wells are drilled on land or offshore on the ocean floor and oil is pumped out. The oil is transported to a refinery by truck, train, or pipeline. There, it is separated into different products such as gasoline, heating oil, diesel fuel, and jet fuel. In 1859, Edwin Drake drilled the first oil well in the United States. Oil was introduced into the fuel market. After the invention of the automobile in the early 1900s, demand for fuel increased.

Natural gas is often found near oil deposits. It is a colorless, odorless gas made mostly of methane. Like oil, natural gas deposits can be on land or under the sea floor. The first company to sell natural gas in the United States was the Fredonia Gas Light Company, founded in 1858 in New York. But with limited technology, the gas was only used locally. Several unsuccessful attempts were made in the late 1800s to transport natural gas. Improved pipeline technology in the 1920s allowed it to be transported over great distances. In the

United States, natural gas production and consumption rose steadily from the 1950s into the 1970s. Most natural gas is used to create heat or electricity.

Why Use Fossil Fuels?

There are several reasons why the world still turns to fossil fuels for energy. Although fossil fuels are nonrenewable, they are still readily available and can be found all over the world. Fossil fuels are also efficient and generate large amounts of energy. Coal, oil, and natural gas are inexpensive. Technological innovations have made extracting, processing, and transporting fossil fuels cheap. The processing or installation costs associated with renewable energies often cannot compete with those of fossil fuels. Also, the modern industrial world was built on a foundation of fossil fuels. Existing industries and transportation systems rely on fossil fuels for power. Transitioning from fossil fuels to renewables will be a slow process.

For more than a century, coal, oil, and natural gas have accounted for more than 80 percent of total US energy consumption. Statistics from 2016 show oil is still king of the fossil fuels. Oil accounted for one-third of global energy consumption. World natural gas production and consumption showed weak growth, but energy company BP noted that "coal's market share fell to 28.1%, the lowest level since 2004."[16] The disadvantages of fossil fuels are changing how the world thinks about its energy sources.

The data indicate the world is transitioning to more renewable energy sources. Despite the availability of cheap fossil fuels, 2015 was a record year for renewable energies. The Renewables 2016 Global Status Report, published by an international group of governments, companies, and organizations interested in renewable energy, showed that the world's fossil fuel consumption reached an all-time high. But it also revealed the highest numbers ever for renewable energy production. Nonfossil fuels, including biomass, are showing growth. The costs of production and installation of renewables has decreased. They are becoming competitive with fossil fuels. Biomass has several advantages over fossil fuels, and while biomass energy also introduces new challenges, researchers are working on ways to resolve these problems.

Fossil fuels' advantages, such as low cost, accessibility, and high energy output, have made them the world's most used sources of energy. Future predictions of global energy consumption show that fossil fuels probably won't lose their prominence anytime soon. In fact, the 2016 edition of the International Energy Outlook, published by the US Energy Information Administration, projects continued reliance on fossil fuels by 2040. It estimated that "in 2040, liquid fuels, natural gas, and coal [will] account for 78% of total world energy consumption."[17] During the same period, global consumption of renewable energies is expected to double. This is due in part to the long-recognized disadvantages of fossil fuels.

Harm to Human Health

Fossil fuels are harmful to humans. Coal mining poses numerous threats to workers, local mining communities, and the environment.

Working conditions are dangerous. Miners may be injured or killed by equipment or collapsing mines. During extraction, explosive gases are released. These gases can cause fires and explosions that endanger miners and residents of local communities. Coal miners also breathe in coal dust and other chemicals that damage their lungs. Loud machinery used in mining causes hearing damage. Residents of nearby communities are also affected by mining. They suffer from increased rates of lung cancer and respiratory ailments. Chemicals from explosives used at mining sites, as well as toxic levels of minerals and heavy metals, contaminate drinking water. In 2010, ABC News explained just how dangerous coal mining can be in the United States: "On average, 50 to 60 coal miners die in this country every year while they work."[18]

The oil and natural gas industries also pose safety and health hazards. Sparks and flames from equipment such as cutting and welding tools or lightning strikes can start fires. Explosions are caused by gases released by wells. Workers are injured or die after falls from elevated platforms. Excavated work spaces are often confined, and workers may breathe in hazardous chemicals, such as hydrogen sulfide gas.

The use of biomass has the potential to be harmful to human health if the proper precautions are not taken. Many people in developing countries burn biomass directly. Traditional fuels such as wood or dried animal dung are burned on open fires or in stoves. This method of energy use, especially when done indoors, can

Raw biomass, such as wood and manure, can be harmful for both the environment and human health when burned directly. Carbon dioxide and other chemicals are released as pollution, while fine dusts or soot created by biomass combustion can cause respiratory issues when inhaled.

have negative health effects, including respiratory and eye ailments. Workers in biomass energy plants face common industrial workplace dangers. Biomass plants have several hazards, such as steam, intense heat and pressure, and machinery noise. Fires and explosions are two of the more common dangers. Health and safety regulations and improvements in safety equipment protect workers and people living near biomass plants. Plants contain equipment to control harmful emissions. Proper training and safety gear, such as respirators and protective garments, ensure that workers are kept safe.

Harm to the Environment

Extracting and using coal, oil, and natural gas are harmful to the environment. Coal can be near Earth's surface or deep underground. Strip mining is one way coal is extracted from the earth. Strip mining damages the landscape by clearing away vegetation, topsoil, and rocks to reach coal deposits just below the surface. Another mining method involves using explosives to remove the tops of mountains. Besides destroying the land, debris from the explosion often gets into nearby water sources. Pollutants enter waterways and are toxic to wildlife. Underground mines are also susceptible to collapse, ruining the land and harming workers. Burning coal is bad for the environment, too. Coal is usually pulverized and then added to a furnace. As water flows through pipes in the furnace, it is heated under pressure. This produces steam that goes to a turbine, which activates a generator to produce electricity. As coal burns, it releases sulfur dioxide, nitrogen oxide, and carbon dioxide gases. These gases pollute the air.

Oil and natural gas industries also have negative impacts on the environment. Drilling for oil has resulted in massive oil spills. One of the largest oil spills in history took place on June 3, 1979, in the Gulf of Mexico. On that day, an exploratory oil well called Ixtoc I exploded. The oil rig caught fire and sank. Over the next ten months, an estimated 126 million gallons (477 million L) of oil gushed into the Gulf of Mexico. Oil spills affect both sea and land ecosystems for many years. After the Ixtoc I incident, many fishers lost their livelihood. Oysters, which were once plentiful in the area, never recovered. One

Oil spills, earthquakes, and pollution can be outcomes of fossil fuel extraction and processing. Researchers are investigating how to limit the environmental impact of biomass energy in order to position it as a viable and more environmentally friendly alternative to fossil fuels.

fisher remembered, "The amount of fish to catch was never the same as before the spill."[19]

Biomass energy also impacts the environment, but with lesser intensity than fossil fuels. Processing biomass does produce some gas emissions, including carbon monoxide, carbon dioxide, and airborne particles. In the United States, the Environmental Protection Agency (EPA) requires that power plants follow strict regulations to control pollution and reduce emissions. Pollutants can be captured using scrubbers, which mix liquid with the gases to neutralize acids, one of the dangerous components of the emissions. Filters remove particles from emissions. The negative effects of any released greenhouse gases are partially counteracted by planting biomass, which captures carbon dioxide from the atmosphere.

Renewability

Another problem with fossil fuels is that they are nonrenewable. Coal, oil, and natural gas were created over a span of millions of years. As human populations increase, worldwide consumption of fossil fuels will keep rising over the next several decades. But there is a finite amount of fossil fuels to feed the need for energy. Supplies of fossil fuels are being depleted. When will stores of coal, oil, and natural gas run out? No one is exactly sure. Some experts anticipate world oil reserves could be used up in the next few decades. And as supplies of fossil fuels lessen, demand and prices will increase. But other oil-industry experts take a different stance. They argue that innovative technologies will help find new reserves and extract the maximum amount of oil and gas. New technologies will also make it possible for oil and gas to be extracted from reserves that are known but currently inaccessible. However, even if there are new fossil fuel reserves to be found, the search and extraction processes will cost time and money.

Climate Change

The biggest concern about fossil fuels is the impact they are having on the climate. Fossil fuels are partially responsible for causing climate change. The term *climate* refers to long-term patterns in weather conditions, such as temperature, precipitation, and humidity. Weather can vary within the same day or from day to day. Climate is the average weather in a region over several years. Changes in Earth's climate are nothing new. Throughout time, there have been several climate cycles. During these cycles Earth's temperatures varied considerably. Some cycles were extremely hot, while others were ice ages, when ice sheets covered much of the planet. Natural climate change is a significant change in temperature, precipitation, and wind patterns over the course of thousands of years.

Earth's atmosphere is made up of layers of gases. Radiation from the Sun passes through the atmosphere. Some of the radiation is reflected back into space by reflective surfaces such as ice, snow, and clouds. Other radiation is absorbed by the world's oceans and land masses, heating the planet. Some of this heat is released back into the atmosphere. Certain types of gases, known as greenhouse gases, prevent some of the reflected radiation from escaping. This results in a warming effect that keeps Earth at a temperature that can sustain life. This natural trapping of heat is known as the greenhouse effect.

Greenhouse gases found in Earth's atmosphere include carbon dioxide, nitrous oxide, and methane. Burning fossil fuels releases these gases into the atmosphere. Adding more greenhouse gases speeds up the greenhouse effect, causing an increase in temperatures on Earth. In the United States, carbon dioxide accounts for most of the country's greenhouse emissions. Between 1990 and 2010, overall emissions of greenhouse gases due to human activity increased by 35 percent. The intensified greenhouse effect has resulted in a warming world. Earth's average temperature has risen by 1.4°F (0.8°C) since 1880. More than half of this warming has happened since 1975.

Climate models predict that if greenhouse emissions continue to increase, Earth's average temperature could rise more than 7.2°F (4°C) by the end of the twenty-first century.

Small changes in Earth's average temperature can have big consequences. The intensity of extreme weather events has been increasing. Record high temperatures cause severe droughts and wildfires. They alter ecosystems, shifting the ranges of wildlife in disruptive or deadly ways. Warming ocean waters produce intense hurricanes and disrupt ecosystems by killing off sea life. Melting snow and polar ice cause rising sea levels. With higher water levels, human populations are displaced by flooding. Tropical diseases spread to new areas as the climate warms, and established patterns of agriculture are changed.

A Biomass Solution

The biomass energy industry offers ways to provide energy without the problems associated with fossil fuels. While the future supply of fossil fuels is limited, biomass is a renewable energy source. Biomass is cheap and readily available. It can come from a variety of sources that are found all over the world. Food crops such as corn, soybeans, and sugarcane can be processed into biofuels. Energy crops, including grasses such as switchgrass and miscanthus, can be grown in mass quantities. Using agricultural and landfill waste, municipal sewage, and animal manure not only produces energy but also rids the planet of garbage. By-products from biomass production are used to manufacture pharmaceutical and cosmetic products.

Middlebury College Achieves Carbon Neutrality

In 2016, Middlebury College announced that it had reached carbon neutrality. The Vermont college succeeded in offsetting the amount of carbon emissions it releases by sequestering carbon. The carbon neutrality plan began in 2001 with an inventory of campus emissions. A large part of the college's success came from using a biomass gasification plant constructed in 2008. Biomass for the plant comes from 24,000 tons (22,000 metric t) of locally sourced wood chips. By using biomass, Middlebury was able to cut its yearly oil consumption from 2 million gallons (7.6 million L) to 600,000 gallons (2.3 million L). The decrease in oil added up to a savings of between $1 million and $2 million a year. The college's president, Laurie Patton, said, "I am thrilled to announce this significant moment in Middlebury's history of environmental leadership. I encourage the campus community to pause and reflect on the importance of this achievement and recognize the visionary work of so many people who brought us to this point." Middlebury is continuing to look for ways it can use cow manure and other biomass to generate energy.

Quoted in "Middlebury Reaches 2016 Carbon Neutrality Goal," *Middlebury Newsroom*, December 8, 2016. middlebury.edu.

Growing plants for biomass energy does not add to levels of atmospheric carbon. When biomass plants are sustainably grown, biomass is carbon neutral. The amount of carbon emitted during harvesting and processing is balanced by the amount of carbon stored by growing new biomass crops. Generating electricity with biomass can often be achieved using the same equipment and power plants that currently use fossil fuels. Biomass can be used as the sole source of energy or used in conjunction with coal or other fossil fuels.

Either way, using biomass to generate energy reduces greenhouse gases and other harmful emissions.

Biomass Challenges: Technical and Financial

Biomass is a promising future energy source. It has several advantages over fossil fuels. But can biomass ever replace fossil fuels as an energy source? First, biomass must overcome some challenges.

Biomass energy's largest problem is **logistics**. Creating a final energy product from biomass requires detailed organization and the implementation of several complex steps. Producing biofuels involves growing, harvesting, processing, transportation, refinement, storage, and distribution. Each step adds to the work and cost of production.

First-generation biofuels are those made from food crops, such as corn. By contrast, second-generation biofuels are made from materials not used for food, such as wood and agricultural waste. They are desirable because they do not compete with food supplies. Also, second-generation biofuels offset substantially more carbon emissions than first-generation biofuels. But second-generation biofuels made from woody biomass require extra processing steps to break down plant tissues and extract and convert sugars into energy. The additional work and complex machinery needed to carry out this processing and create second-generation biofuels drives up production costs. Some estimates show that producing second-generation biofuels can be two to three times more expensive than the production of oil. Converting biomass to usable energy can be a rigorous and costly undertaking that makes producing and selling biofuels an uphill battle. But advancing technologies hold the promise of making bioenergy production more streamlined, efficient, and cost-competitive in the future.

Biomass Challenges: Ethical

Biomass energy production is faced with a major ethical question: Does biofuel production threaten the world's food supply? Bioenergy has low energy density. This means that large volumes of biomass are required to produce energy. Producing bioenergy requires using vast areas of land to grow feedstock. The biofuel industry has been criticized for using land that might otherwise have been used to grow crops for food. Human populations are growing and depleting land that can be used for agriculture. Some people are concerned that using land and growing crops for fuel will cause food shortages for the world's poor communities. They also contend that using food crops for biofuels will drive up food prices. Tim Searchinger is a senior fellow at the World Resources Institute and a research scholar and lecturer at Princeton University. He warns against using land to produce bioenergy: "Even modest quantities of bioenergy would greatly increase the global competition for land. People already use roughly three-quarters of the world's vegetated land for crops, livestock grazing, and wood harvests."[20]

Trouble began brewing in 2008, when reports were published that blamed a steep rise in world food prices on the production of biofuels. The argument stated that biofuels compete for land and food crops and displace food production, thereby driving up the price of food. However, a 2016 report released by the Renewable Fuels Association found that "retail food prices were not impacted in any demonstrable way by expansion of U.S. grain ethanol production."[21] The connection between bioenergy production, land use, and food security is complex and involves many factors.

Government Policy Affects Biomass Energy

The US federal government can affect the energy market. Government policies influence whether biomass energy will ever be able to replace energy derived from fossil fuels. For almost a century, the US government has supported the research, development, and production of fossil fuels. Tax benefits given to oil and gas industries promote the production of oil and gas in the United States. These **subsidies** keep down production and development costs

and help keep prices lower for consumers. In the 1980s, Congress began subsidizing ethanol in order to reduce the country's reliance on foreign oil. The Energy Policy Act (EPAct) of 2005 added federal incentives to favor renewable energy. The EPAct implemented the Renewable Fuel Standard (RFS) program. As the Department of Energy explains, "The RFS requires renewable fuel to be blended into transportation fuel in increasing amounts each year, escalating to 36 billion gallons (136 billion L) by 2022."[22] The goal of the RFS program is to reduce greenhouse gas emissions and reduce the country's reliance on imported oil. In recent years, subsidies for renewable energies have increased dramatically. In March 2017, the Congressional Budget Office (CBO) reported that "an estimated $10.9 billion . . . was directed toward renewable energy."[23] Just $4.6 billion went to fossil fuels. Many states have their own renewable fuel standards and offer programs that encourage the production and use of biomass fuels. Such government policies may help biomass energy become more cost-competitive with fossil fuels.

HOW DOES BIOMASS IMPACT THE ENVIRONMENT?

Biomass has the potential to reduce worldwide dependence on fossil fuels. Increased use of biomass as an energy source can also cut greenhouse gas emissions and make use of waste materials. Sources of biomass ranging from woods to grasses to waste can be processed in various ways. Biomass can be converted into liquids, solids, and gases, making it a versatile energy source. Despite these positive attributes, biomass energy production and use remains controversial. Certain types of biomass, as well as the places and methods used for growing, harvesting, and processing them, may be beneficial in one case and detrimental in another.

There are particular characteristics that make a biomass source beneficial. First, it must be renewable and sustainable. This means the source must be grown, harvested, and processed in a way that has a minimum negative impact on the environment. Growing crops and harvesting wood from forests must not destroy habitats or compete for land with food crops. To become a feasible fuel, biomass must be produced in abundant amounts to support heat, electrical, and transportation needs. Biomass energy technologies also need to make economic sense.

Is Biomass Renewable and Sustainable?

Biomass is a renewable energy source. Biomass sources from plants derive their energy from the Sun and can be regrown in a relatively short period of time. Waste feedstocks are constantly being produced. However, just because a source is renewable does not mean it is also sustainable. The type of biomass and the practices used to grow and harvest biomass can have an impact on the land. Some biomass production can cause degradation of the environment. Improper farming and management techniques can make biomass energy unsustainable. Crops may be planted and harvested in ways that damage ecosystems. Biofuel crop farming practices are sometimes driven by market demand for biomass. A demand for energy crops can result in farmers expanding crops into lands set aside for conservation purposes. Growing biomass crops on these lands alters habitats and means that certain kinds of plants and animals may not survive in the area. In the United States, some farmers are paid to keep environmentally sensitive parcels of land free from crops.

Growing biomass crops can require large volumes of water. The amount of water used depends on the types and amounts of crops grown as well as the type of land being used. For example, drier

Miscanthus and other energy crops can be grown in vast quantities for biomass energy production. But some people question whether so much land should be set aside for energy crops when it could be used for food production.

land requires more frequent irrigation and larger quantities of water. Farmers' use of pesticides, herbicides, and fertilizers affects water quality. Fertilizers contain large amounts of nitrogen that can wash into bodies of water such as rivers. Excess nitrogen in bodies of water can create oxygen-poor areas known as dead zones, resulting in the death of aquatic life. Other water-related problems can be triggered by soil erosion. This process occurs when land is used repeatedly to grow crops. Row crops used in ethanol production, such as corn, are known to produce more sediment than other crops. Soil sediments can carry pollutants into water sources and harm water quality.

Smart farming and management practices ensure that negative impacts on the land will be reduced or eliminated. Biomass feedstock crops must be carefully chosen for characteristics that make them renewable and sustainable. Scientists conduct studies of the life cycle of biomass crops and their pathways to fuel to determine the environmental impact of various types of biomass sources.

Research is focused on developing and improving biomass crops that are renewable and sustainable. Perennial grasses grown specifically as energy crops hold promise. These include varieties of switchgrass that are native to the United States, as well as nonnative miscanthus from Japan and eastern Asia. Perennial grasses are favored as energy crops for several reasons. They are fast-growing and easy to grow. They do not have to be replanted every year, instead regrowing from their roots. This saves both time and money. Once established, perennial grasses require little input of fertilizers, pesticides, and water, especially when compared with first-generation feedstocks such as corn. Planting grasses that are regionally native means they are already adapted to local conditions and require little management to grow.

Using native plants also ensures that growing and processing remain sustainable. Grasses can grow in areas that are not suitable for growing food crops. They can tolerate dry, rocky, or poor soil conditions. Their roots grow deep into the soil, preventing erosion. Most grasses are high-yield crops. Once harvested, grasses can be converted into pellets, briquettes, and other compressed forms.

This makes them convenient to transfer and store. Compressed biomass also burns more efficiently. Using perennial grasses has an additional benefit to local ecology. Studies show that perennial grass crops provide habitats for many kinds of birds. The University of Iowa explains that such crops also "produce flowers and seeds, which improve wildlife habitat."[24]

Is Biomass Carbon Neutral?

As plants grow and carry out photosynthesis, they remove carbon dioxide from the atmosphere. The plants then store the carbon. When the biomass is burned as fuel, an equal amount of carbon dioxide is released into the atmosphere. The result is that biomass does not add to the carbon dioxide already present in the atmosphere.

The Willow Biomass Project

The Willow Biomass Project is an effort in New York State to grow shrub willow trees for biomass energy production. The State University of New York College of Environmental Science and Forestry and more than twenty other organizations have partnered to research and develop shrub willow trees for biomass energy. More than 1,250 acres (500 ha) of land have been planted. Willows make an ideal biomass for several reasons. They are a short-rotation crop that grows easily and quickly in poor soil. Willows resprout after being cut and can be harvested every three years. The trees produce a large amount of biomass. There are other environmental benefits to planting willows. They remove pollutants from soil and reduce soil erosion. Willows also create habitat for wildlife. As the college explains, "Willow systems can be multifunctional and produce sustainable energy along with other value-added benefits to ecosystems and communities."

Quoted in "The Willow Project at SUNY-ESF," *State University of New York*, n.d. esf.edu.

This scenario represents ideal conditions. In reality, there are a number of factors that alter the balance of carbon absorbed and released. Fossil fuel energy is often used to run machinery during the planting, harvesting, transporting, processing, and distribution of biomass fuels. The emissions from this energy production are not offset. Altering the landscape also impacts the carbon neutrality of biomass production. Overall, the carbon neutrality of biomass is difficult to assess. The *New York Times* examined this controversy. On one side, it explained, "It makes sense not to count carbon dioxide from burning trees when the trees will grow back and recapture all the carbon released when they were burned."[25] However, the article adds, "It takes many decades for seedlings to grow into trees and recapture all the carbon emitted."[26]

Deforestation and Carbon Neutrality

Scientists and environmentalists are concerned that the wood biomass industry is causing more harm than good. In fact, the growing desire for wood biomass is leading to deforestation in some parts of the world. Removing trees for wood feedstock is not a carbon neutral practice. Land cleared of trees does not absorb nearly as much carbon as forests, especially old growth forests that have existed for one hundred or more years. And as the biomass fuel from the cleared forests is burned, it adds carbon to the atmosphere.

Trees have long been recognized for being excellent at storing carbon in their wood. While some carbon is lost as trees die and decay, healthy forests store far more carbon than they release.

Deforestation is one obstacle to biomass energy achieving carbon neutrality. Cutting down trees reduces the landscape's ability to absorb carbon.

Trees live for many years and therefore store carbon for a long period of time. As NASA explains, "Forests and other land vegetation currently remove up to 30 percent of human carbon dioxide emissions from the atmosphere during photosynthesis."[27] Large losses of trees can have a major impact on the levels of carbon dioxide in the atmosphere, speeding up climate change.

Historically, wood has been the most used of all biomass sources worldwide. According to the Food and Agriculture Organization of the United Nations, more than 2 billion people rely on wood energy for cooking and heating. This is especially true in developing countries. In the United States, wood biomass is still used to generate heat in some homes, commercial buildings, and industries. Wood biomass is also used to generate electrical power. Forests in many regions of the world are affected by the increased demand for biomass.

The wood biomass industry in the United States is booming, particularly in the Southeast. Enviva Holdings of North Carolina is the world's largest producer of wood pellets. It owns and operates wood pellet plants throughout the southeastern United States and produces almost 3.3 million tons (3 million metric t) of pellets per year. Most of the pellets are exported to the United Kingdom and Europe. There, the pellets fuel power plants that once burned coal. The rising demand for wood pellets in Europe resulted from the European Commission's 2020 climate and energy plan. The plan calls for reduced greenhouse gas emissions and increased use of renewable energy. The commission classifies wood pellets as carbon neutral; this allows wood pellets to help nations reach their renewable energy targets. European governments provide subsidies to companies to encourage the use of biomass as a fuel source. The Drax power plant in north-central England uses a huge percentage of US and Canadian wood pellet exports to the United Kingdom. The US Energy Information Administration notes, "In 2014, the Drax plant's wood pellet supply alone accounted for more than 80% of all of the United Kingdom's wood pellet imports from the United States, and almost 60% of all US wood pellet exports to all countries."[28] Drax co-fires wood pellets with coal to generate electricity.

Wood Controversy

Pellets are primarily composed of waste wood. But environmentalists believe that there is not sufficient waste wood to meet industry demand. They argue that the growing market for pellets is driving pellet companies to harvest whole trees. The National Resources Defense Council (NRDC) contends that wood pellet manufacturers in the mid-Atlantic and southeast United States harvest whole trees from private land to produce pellets. They point out that states in these regions have weak or nonexistent restrictions and regulations regarding forestry practices. The NRDC says, "This massive additional demand for logs now risks destroying ecosystems that can never be replaced."[29] The group says that federal laws that apply to forestry operations are ambiguous and inconsistent.

Cutting hardwood trees creates a carbon deficit. Removing trees, processing them into pellets, and burning them for fuel releases greenhouse gases. Harvesting whole trees also means there are fewer trees to sequester carbon. Replanting trees does not balance out the effects of taking down mature trees. Young trees simply do not have the carbon storage capacity of older trees. In their report, "The Great American Stand: US Forests & The Climate Emergency," climate scientist Dr. William Moomaw and Danna Smith, the executive director of an environmental nonprofit organization, advocated for increased protection of American forests. They argued that bioenergy should not be described as carbon neutral:

Burning trees in place of fossil fuels for energy will accelerate, not reduce, carbon emissions while also degrading forests' ability to provide critical climate mitigation and other ecosystem services. Efforts to characterize bioenergy or other wood products as "carbon neutral" are not only inaccurate, but irrelevant. "Carbon neutrality" is not good enough because concentrations of carbon dioxide in the atmosphere must decrease rather than remain constant over time.[30]

Other environmental groups, including the Center for Biological Diversity, Global Forest Coalition, and Friends of the Earth International also strongly oppose harvesting trees from natural forests.

The debate about wood biomass as a carbon neutral, sustainable feedstock continues. Wood biomass industry leaders maintain that their practices are sustainable, low carbon or carbon neutral, and a cleaner alternative to fossil fuels. Many experts agree. Forest manager William Stewart is codirector of the Center for Forestry, Agriculture, and Natural Resources at the University of California, Berkeley. He believes that proper tree harvesting is beneficial. "Forests have been harvested for bioenergy long before it became a controversy. They benefit from thinning, and they are healthier because there is less competition for water and nutrients."[31] The Nature Conservancy and World Resources Institute agree. Both organizations advocate for sustainable forest management.

International Biofuels

Demand for biofuels as an alternative energy source is having an impact on environments outside the United States as well. Tropical forests in South America and Southeast Asia have been especially affected by the biofuel industry. The demand for these fuels is growing as more countries strive to achieve lowered greenhouse gas emissions and lessen their dependence on fossil fuels. Global biofuel production increased by 3 percent between 2014 and 2015. In 2015, 35 billion gallons (132 billion L) of biofuel were produced worldwide. While burning biofuels is cleaner than burning fossil fuels, biofuel feedstock production poses a threat to forests and other ecosystems.

Brazil is a leader in the production of ethanol from sugarcane. Interest in biofuels was sparked in the 1970s, following an oil crisis that highlighted the country's dependence on foreign sources of oil. The country set aside large amounts of land for growing sugarcane. By the 2010s, more than 1 million people worked in the nation's sugarcane industry. About 96 percent of Brazil's cars were capable of running on ethanol or a blend of ethanol and gasoline.

Biodiesel is another type of biofuel derived from plant oils. Experts forecast that between 2016 and 2020, biodiesel production and consumption will increase 14 percent. Production in 2020 is expected to reach 10 billion gallons (38 billion L), up from 8.8 billion gallons (33.3 billion L) in 2016. Biodiesel is commonly made from soy and palm oils sourced in tropical regions. Production of such biodiesel is contributing to a decline in tropical forest habitat.

On the island of Borneo in Indonesia, farmers tend palm oil trees grown on massive plantations called **monocultures**. Years ago, the plantations were lush with tropical forest vegetation and abundant wildlife. But the rain forests have been cleared and burned to grow and harvest profitable palm fruit. Palm oil fruit produces high yields of oil and is inexpensive to produce. Indonesia and Malaysia account for about 80 percent of worldwide production. Other countries in South America and Africa are home to palm oil plantations as well. The deforestation of tropical forests is having a major impact on carbon storage. Tropical forests cover only about 6 or 7 percent of dry land on Earth. Yet they are capable of significant carbon storage.

Moist peat lands in Southeast Asia have also fallen prey to palm oil interests. Peat is well-known for its ability to store large amounts of carbon. Wet peat lands are drained in order to plant palm oil trees, which cannot be grown in soggy land. Destroying peat lands releases carbon and wipes out vast areas where carbon can be sequestered. Studies have shown that deforestation of tropical forests is the second greatest contributor to greenhouse emissions behind burning fossil fuels. When carbon emissions due to deforestation and the destruction of peat lands are accounted for, the production of biodiesel from palm oil emits more greenhouse gas than fossil fuels. Many governments are now rethinking their stance on biofuels derived from palm and other plant oils.

Reducing Impacts

Countries worldwide are pursuing several approaches to lessen the impact of the bioenergy industry on the environment. Biomass industries are developing tracking systems that ensure biomass is being harvested responsibly without damaging the environment. US wood pellet producer Enviva has implemented a "Track and Trace" system to verify where its wood biomass is coming from. The company describes what kind of information it receives:

> With Track & Trace, we record the geographic location, age, and forest type for all of our primary wood. We know how and by whom each tract was harvested, as well as the proportion of wood that was sent to Enviva versus other forest products industry consumers.[35]

Enviva says it will not accept wood from suppliers who do not provide detailed information about the specific tract of forest where wood is harvested. The tracking system ensures that wood is sustainably sourced and US forests are protected from deforestation.

In April 2017, the European Parliament issued a statement asking the European Union to devise a single certification plan for palm oil being imported into the European Union. Current sustainability certification rules were seen as insufficient and confusing. The parliament also suggested that the use of vegetable oils that cause deforestation, especially palm oil, be phased out by 2020. Forty-six percent of the palm oil imported by the European Union is used for biofuels. As with wood sources, sources of palm oil

Life Cycle Assessments

Life cycle assessments (LCAs) are also called "cradle-to-grave" analyses. LCAs examine the impact a certain source of biomass will have on the environment and on human health throughout its life cycle. LCAs provide a way to determine if a biomass is sustainable and carbon neutral. Researchers study the ways that a biomass can affect the environment. They consider the amount of energy and materials needed to grow, harvest, process, transport, use, and dispose of the biomass and any products associated with it. Estimations are made about greenhouse gases that will be emitted during the life of the biomass source. Scientists also consider the effects that pollutants such as particles and toxic gases may have on human health. LCAs are useful for identifying the positive environmental potential of a biomass source. At the same time, negative environmental impacts can be recognized and addressed. LCAs evaluate the value of biomass feedstocks and methods of processing. After conducting an LCA, people can make educated decisions about a biomass source and whether it is sustainable and carbon neutral.

would be traced to ensure the oil was coming from land that meets sustainability standards.

Ongoing research is investigating better ways to process waste sources of biomass into usable fuels. Using waste as feedstock reduces the need to harvest whole live trees and disrupt ecosystems. A team of investigators at the University of Washington has converted wood from trees killed by beetle infestations into bio-oil. The dead trees pose a threat from falling and are a fire hazard. The damaged wood cannot be used for lumber. Using pyrolysis, the researchers made bio-oil which can then be upgraded into fuels for transportation. The process is even more efficient and cost-effective because the wood can be processed where it is found using mobile reactors. Researchers continue to develop energy crops that can be harvested and processed more efficiently without adding to carbon emissions.

Does Biomass Energy Cause Pollution?

On September 13, 2016, a group of medical and public health officials in the United States sent a letter to the EPA detailing the health risks associated with biomass burning. The letter, signed by members of the American Academy of Pediatrics, the Allergy and Asthma Network, the American Lung Association, and other medical professionals specifically targeted the use of biomass for generating electricity. They detailed the health problems associated with burning biomass, such as asthma, cardiovascular disease, and lung cancer. The health issues are caused by pollution.

All biomass sources create pollution. The amount and type of pollution varies depending on the type of biomass, how it is produced, and how it is used for fuel. Biomass produces harmful emissions such as carbon dioxide, carbon monoxide, sulfur dioxide, and nitrogen oxides. Fine dusts, or particulates, are another harmful by-product of biomass combustion. Burning raw biomass, such as wood, produces the highest amount of pollution. As wood burns, it produces carbon dioxide and water, along with heat. Burning wood also releases carbon monoxide, nitrogen dioxide, soot particles, and hundreds of toxic chemicals. Inhaled particles and chemicals enter nasal passages and lungs. They cause respiratory ailments ranging from membrane irritation to lung cancer.

Even though they burn more cleanly and give off fewer emissions than pure gasoline and diesel fuel, liquid biofuels such as ethanol and biodiesel do release some harmful emissions into the air. In particular, ethanol and biodiesel have higher evaporative emissions. Evaporative emissions are vapors given off from tanks that store biofuels. Some vapors are also released from pumps and other equipment used to dispense biofuels. Evaporative emissions contribute to smog and harmful ground-level ozone. The multistep production of ethanol is also a source of pollution. Several pollutants are released during each stage of production, from fermentation and distillation to storage.

Common contaminants include acetaldehyde and formaldehyde. Exposure to acetaldehyde causes respiratory irritation. Both it and formaldehyde are considered **carcinogens**.

> ## WORDS IN CONTEXT
> **carcinogens**
> Substances that can cause cancer.

The US government has outlined strict regulations for pollution control. These regulations limit the amount of pollutants that are released into the atmosphere or environment from biomass energy. Emissions control requirements vary according to the type of biomass source used.

In 1970, Congress established the Clean Air Act in response to smog-shrouded cities around the nation. New scientific data about the threats of acid rain and the damaged ozone layer led to revisions to improve the act in 1977 and 1990. The act requires the EPA to set air

At the McNeil Generating Station in Burlington, Vermont, equipment such as scrubbers and filters reduce the gasification plant's emissions. The emissions are cut to one-tenth the level allowed by state law.

quality standards for common pollutants. These include particle pollution, ozone, sulfur dioxide, nitrogen dioxide, carbon monoxide, and lead. Each state has a plan to meet and maintain air quality standards. The standards concern emissions from cars, power plants, and industries. Sources of pollution such as power plants and industries must be built with the latest technology to meet air quality standards. The act also covers greenhouse gases. To set standards, the EPA collects and analyzes information about air pollution and its effects from scientists and other experts.

Biomass processing plants are equipped with pollution control devices to remove impurities and harmful emissions. Devices include scrubbers, fabric filters, and electrostatic air cleaners. Electrostatic air cleaners give an electric charge to particles of toxic materials found in dust or gases as they pass into the exhaust system. The particles are deposited on collection plates. The particles fall off and are collected and removed. **Activated charcoal** blown into power plant exhaust systems binds with toxic elements such as mercury. The resulting clumps of matter are caught in exhaust system filters. Ethanol plants use scrubbers to reduce harmful emissions. Water mixed with chemicals is sprayed into

WORDS IN CONTEXT

activated charcoal
Charcoal processed to have many small pores.

polluted air before it is vented. Some pollutants dissolve into the water while others bind to the chemicals. The clean air is vented from the plant and the wastewater is collected for removal or to be converted into usable compounds. These technological steps, along with well-informed policy decisions, can help reduce the impacts of biomass energy on the environment.

CHAPTER 4

WHAT IS THE FUTURE OF
BIOM*A*SS ENERGY?

Biomass power remains a small part of global energy production. One of the major obstacles is in being able to produce bioenergy on a commercial scale and make it less expensive than fossil fuels. Nations around the world are recognizing the need to reduce reliance on fossil fuels and slow climate change by reducing carbon emissions. Biomass energy, along with renewable energy sources such as solar and wind, can help meet these goals. Nations are setting biomass energy targets to spur research.

In the United States, the Energy Independence and Security Act (EISA) of 2007 requires improvements in vehicle gas mileage and expanded use of renewable energy sources, including biofuels. The EPA noted that one of its goals was to "increase the production of clean renewable fuels."[33] One US report on biomass spoke about the potential of this energy source: "Recognizing this great potential, attention then logically turns to questions of how to mobilize this resource. While bioenergy currently is the greatest single source of renewable energy in the United States, there are still economic and technological barriers that limit efforts to mobilize biomass resources for more biofuels, biopower, and bioproducts."[34]

Feedstock Development

Scientists are researching new sources of biomass. The trend is turning away from first-generation feedstocks such as corn. First-generation feedstocks have a number of issues that make them less desirable than second-generation feedstocks. Growing crops such as corn requires large tracts of land and substantial input to produce a worthwhile yield. In many cases, it requires a great deal of energy to produce a feedstock, with little energy generated in return.

Biofuel for Jets

As airplanes fly, they produce contrails. These are line-shaped clouds produced when hot engine exhaust mixes with cold air several miles above Earth's surface. Contrails are made of ice crystals frozen around soot and metal particles in the aircraft's exhaust. Contrails also contain harmful emissions such as carbon dioxide, carbon monoxide, and methane. Researchers believe that contrails affect Earth's environment because the clouds can remain in the atmosphere for a long time and can cover a large area. In an effort to reduce aircraft contrail emissions, NASA conducted tests using biofuels to power aircraft. Researcher Rich Moore explained why the study was so pioneering: "This was the first time we have quantified the amount of soot particles emitted by jet engines while burning a 50-50 blend of biofuel in flight." The results showed that biofuels substantially decrease aircraft exhaust particles, reducing their soot emissions by 50 to 70 percent.

Quoted in "NASA Study Confirms Biofuels Reduce Jet Engine Pollution," *NASA*, April 24, 2017. nasa.gov.

The energy needed to produce and process first-generation biomass may contribute to climate change instead of reducing it. Researcher Jason Hill explains, "It's true that our first-generation biofuels have not lived up to their promise. We've found they do not offer the environmental benefits they were purported to have, and they have a substantial negative impact on the food system."[35]

Lignocellulosic Biomass

Research is focused on developing new technologies that create biomass sources that are reliable, economical, and sustainable. Lignocellulosic biomass is one of the most promising feedstocks and may have the potential to replace fossil fuels. Lignocellulosic biomass is not made from food crops. It consists of plant waste from crops, wood, and other industries. Lignocellulosic biomass is derived from the cell walls of plants. The cell walls are made up of molecules of lignin, hemicellulose, and cellulose. These components are what give plants their structure. They make plants rigid and strong and help them grow upward against gravity.

Lignocellulosic biomass has several advantages over first-generation feedstocks. Plant waste for feedstock is plentiful and inexpensive. Lignocellulosic biomass can also come from specially grown crops, such as grasses, that can be grown on **marginal** lands where food crops cannot be grown. Lignocellulosic energy

Lignocellulosic biomass energy has the potential to turn plant waste products into commercial ethanol. Bioethanol research seeks to refine the treatment process for plant waste to ensure it is an economically viable source of energy.

crops cost less to grow, harvest, and convert, and they do not compete with food markets.

However, lignocellulosic biomass does have limitations that need to be overcome in order for cellulosic ethanol to be made commercially. Lignocellulose is a tough material to break down. It is this toughness that makes it difficult to convert lignocellulosic biomass to fuel without pretreatments. These added treatments increase the price of producing fuels. Chemical composition and other variations in cellulosic biomass make it difficult to process efficiently and effectively. Differences in local growing conditions, harvesting methods, and even weather conditions can all affect the end product.

Expectations are high for this source of biomass energy. Sandia National Labs describes lignocellulosic biomass as "one of the most abundant plants on Earth and . . . a critical feedstock for the production of renewable fuels."[36] Researchers are studying feedstock sources, harvest times and methods, and treatment processes in order to produce high-quality products that can be created in large quantities.

Algal Biomass

Algae are simple life forms that have tremendous potential for producing biofuels. Algae are a diverse group of organisms. They range from microscopic cyanobacteria to giant kelp. Some algae convert sunlight into energy that is stored as oil. The biggest benefit of using algae as a feedstock is that their growth rate is more than twenty times higher than that of typical feedstock crops. Massive amounts of algae can be grown, harvested, and processed into fuel. The US Department of Energy estimates that "algae could potentially produce up to 60 times more oil per acre than land-based plants."[37] As they grow, algae remove carbon dioxide from the atmosphere.

Private companies are studying algae biology. Their aim is to produce algae that grow quickly and have increased oil content. Companies are working with private universities to try to better understand photosynthesis in algae to increase biofuel production. The research produced by one such collaboration, between Exxon Mobil and the Massachusetts Institute of Technology, suggested that "if key research hurdles are overcome, algal biofuels will have about 50% lower life cycle greenhouse gas emissions than petroleum-derived fuel."[38]

Waste Biomass

There is a growing interest in converting waste to energy. The US Office of Energy Efficiency & Renewable Energy recognizes wet, solid, and gaseous wastes as significant feedstocks for producing biofuels, biogas, heat, and electricity. Waste can come from a number of sources such as wastewater, animal manure, inedible fats and greases, and food. Using waste streams has the added benefit of ridding the environment of pollutants. The Bioenergy Technologies Office (BETO), part of the Department of Energy, published a report in January 2017 that focused on the production of biofuels and other products from wet and gaseous waste sources. The report discussed the potential of waste sources as an energy source. In the United States, it noted, about 50 million tons (45 million metric t) of waste per year are "available for conversion to biofuels, bioproducts, or biopower."[39]

Improving Conversion Technologies

Developing better feedstocks is just one step to ensuring that biofuels can become a future source of global energy. Advanced conversion technologies are needed to efficiently change biomass to biofuels. One way researchers are improving this process is through genetic engineering, also called **bioengineering**. Bioengineered organisms can be tailored to process molecules in more useful ways. In genetic engineering, scientists

WORDS IN CONTEXT

bioengineering
Using biological techniques to change an organism.

69

manipulate an organism's genetic material. By turning genes on and off, scientists change the way organisms grow and function. Bioengineered microbes are improving how cellulose is processed into fuel. In 2014, researchers at the University of Georgia and the BioEnergy Science Center at Oak Ridge National Laboratory added a gene to a bacteria known for its ability to break down lignin. The added gene enabled the bacterium to ferment simple sugars into ethanol. When modified bacteria were added to raw switchgrass, they broke down the plant's cellulose and converted 70 percent of its sugars to ethanol. The goal is to raise that figure to at least 90 percent. One of the geneticists on the project, Janet Westpheling, explained the benefit of using organisms that can naturally break down lignin: "If you start with organisms that can do the hard part, teaching them to make ethanol is relatively easy."[40]

More recently, a "super yeast" was engineered to ferment a plant sugar that normally goes to waste during biofuel production. The yeast researchers used, *Saccharomyces cerevisiae*, is commonly used to ferment sugars to alcohol. But the yeast does not eat xylose, a sugar that sometimes makes up almost 50 percent of plant sugars. By providing the yeast with only xylose to eat, scientists forced the yeast to adapt to ferment xylose. Researcher Trey Sato said this work could have a widespread impact: "If we know how to better metabolize carbon, including xylose, anybody in theory should be able to rewire or change metabolic pathways to produce a variety of biofuel products."[41]

Biomass: The Energy of the Future

Renewable biomass gets its energy from organic material. It is the oldest energy source used by humans. Through photosynthesis, plants harness energy from the Sun and store it as chemical energy. That energy can be released by direct burning to create heat. Biomass can also be processed to create liquid or gas fuels. Wood was people's primary source of biomass energy in ancient times, and it remained the main source of fuel in rural US areas until the early 1900s. The discovery of oil and natural gas, along with new technologies for transporting and using them, helped popularize the use of these fossil fuels in the United States. Fossil fuels remain popular and are still the most consumed fuels today. They are readily available and easy to use, and they release high amounts of energy.

However, changes in the energy industry are happening fast. Researchers have recognized the dangers of extracting and burning fossil fuels. Companies and governments are searching for alternative, renewable energy technologies. Biomass energy is one of them. Technological advances have made biomass an attractive energy option. Thanks to the work of researchers, it is now possible to create energy-rich, sustainable feedstocks that produce environmentally friendly fuels.

INTRODUCTION: POWERED BY BIOMASS

1. Quoted in Martha C. Monroe, "Co-firing with Wood and Sugarcane Waste," *eXtension*, March 12, 2010. articles.extension.org.

2. Quoted in "Fla. Plant to Use Sugar to Generate Electricity," *JOC*, February 17, 1994. joc.com.

3. Quoted in Ted West, "The Vegetable-Oil Alternative," *Car and Driver*, March 2004. caranddriver.com.

4. Quoted in "Energy from Municipal Waste," *US Energy Information Administration*, November 2016. eia.gov.

5. Quoted in "2016 Billion-Ton Report," *US Department of Energy*, July 2016. energy.gov.

CHAPTER 1: HOW DOES BIOMASS ENERGY WORK?

6. Quoted in "Nonrenewable and Renewable Energy Sources," *US Energy Information Administration*, n.d. eia.gov.

7. Quoted in Holli Riebeek, "The Carbon Cycle," *Earth Observatory*, June 16, 2011. earthobservatory.nasa.gov.

8. Quoted in James Quinn, "Why Biomass Is Key to the UK's Energy Future," *Telegraph*, November 4, 2014. Telegraph.co.uk.

9. "2017 BioenergizeMe Infographic Challenge: Hydrothermal Liquefaction of Algae," *US Department of Energy*, n.d. energy.gov.

10. Quoted in Andy Koss, "Our Biomass Units Deliver 80 Percent Carbon Savings Compared to Coal," *Somerset County Gazette*, June 19, 2017. somersetcountygazette.co.uk.

11. Quoted in "Fueling a High Octane Future," *Renewable Fuels Association*, February 2016. ethanolrfa.org.

12. Quoted in "Fueling a High Octane Future."

13. Quoted in "Meet an Anaerobic Digester Operator," *Environmental Protection Agency*, May 2016. epa.gov.

14. Quoted in "Ethanol Fuel Basics," *US Department of Energy*, n.d. afdc.energy.gov.

CHAPTER 2: CAN BIOMASS ENERGY REPLACE FOSSIL FUELS?

15. Quoted in "Coal Explained," *US Energy Information Administration*, n.d. eia.gov.

16. Quoted in "BP Statistical Review of World Energy June 2017," *Beyond Petroleum*, June 2017. bp.com.

17. Quoted in "World Energy Demand and Economic Outlook," *US Energy Information Administration*, 2016. eia.gov.

18. Quoted in David Kerley and Michael Murray, "Mining: The Most Dangerous Job?" *ABC News*, April 6, 2010. abcnews.go.com.

19. Quoted in Julian Miglierini, "Mexicans Still Haunted by 1979 Ixtoc Spill," *BBC*, June 14, 2010. bbc.com.

20. Quoted in Tim Searchinger, "Why Dedicating Land to Bioenergy Won't Curb Climate Change," *World Resources Institute*, January 28, 2015. wri.org.

21. Quoted in "The Impact of Ethanol Industry Expansion on Food Prices: A Retrospective Analysis," *Renewable Fuels Association*, November 2016. ethanolrfa.org.

22. Quoted in "Renewable Fuel Standard," *US Department of Energy*, n.d. afdc.energy.gov.

23. "Federal Support for Developing, Producing, and Using Fuels and Energy Technologies," *Congressional Budget Office*, March 29, 2017. cbo.gov.

CHAPTER 3: HOW DOES BIOMASS IMPACT THE ENVIRONMENT?

24. Quoted in "Miscanthus Biomass Fuel Project," *Sustainability*, n.d. sustainability.uiowa.edu.

25. Quoted in Eduardo Porter, "Next 'Renewable Energy': Burning Forests, If Senators Get Their Way."

26. Quoted in Carol Rasmussen, "NASA Finds Good News on Forests and Carbon Dioxide," *NASA*, December 29, 2014. nasa.gov.

27. Quoted in "NASA Finds Good News on Forests and Carbon Dioxide."

28. Quoted in "UK's Renewable Energy Targets Drive Increases in US Wood Pellet Exports," *US Energy Information Administration*, April 22, 2015. eia.gov.

29. Quoted in "The Truth about the Biomass Industry: How Wood Pellet Exports Pollute Our Climate and Damage Our Forests," *Natural Resource Defense Council*, August 2014. nrdc.org.

30. Quoted in "The Great American Stand," *Dogwood Alliance*, March 21, 2017. dogwoodalliance.org.

31. Quoted in Judith Horstman, "Forest Bioenergy: Is It Sustainable?" *Bioenergy Connection*, 2013. bioenergyconnection.org.

32. Quoted in "Track & Trace," *Enviva*, n.d. envivabiomass.com.

CHAPTER 4: WHAT IS THE FUTURE OF BIOMASS ENERGY?

33. Quoted in "Summary of the Energy Independence and Security Act," *Environmental Protection Agency*, n.d. epa.gov.

34. Quoted in "2016 Billion-Ton Report."

35. Quoted in Justin Gillis, "New Report Urges Western Governments to Reconsider Reliance on Biofuels," *New York Times*, January 28, 2015. nytimes.com.

36. Quoted in "Lignocellulosic Biomass," *Sandia National Laboratories*, n.d. energy.sandia.gov.

37. Quoted in "Energy 101: Algae-to-Fuel," *US Department of Energy*, n.d. energy.gov.

38. Quoted in "Advanced Biofuels," *ExxonMobil*, n.d. exxonmobil.com.

39. Quoted in "Biofuels and Bioproducts from Wet and Gaseous Waste Streams: Challenges and Opportunities," *US Department of Energy*, January 2017. energy.gov.

40. Quoted in Robert F. Service, "Unusual Microbe Engineered to Convert Grass to Gas," *Science*, June 2, 2014. sciencemag.org.

41. Quoted in "'Super Yeast' Has the Power to Improve Economics of Biofuels," *Biomass Magazine*, October 19, 2016. biomassmagazine.com.

BOOKS

John Allen, *Careers in Environmental and Energy Technology.* San Diego, CA: ReferencePoint, 2017.

William Dudley, *Biofuels.* San Diego, CA: ReferencePoint, 2016.

Carol Hand, *Biomass Energy.* Minneapolis, MN: Abdo Publishing, 2013.

Terry Allan Hicks, *The Pros and Cons of Biofuel.* New York: Cavendish Square, 2015.

Paula Johanson, *Biofuels: Sustainable Energy in the 21st Century.* New York: Rosen Publishing, 2010.

Stuart A. Kallen, *Cutting Edge Energy Technology.* San Diego, CA: ReferencePoint, 2017.

Carla Mooney, *What Is the Future of Biofuels?* San Diego, CA: ReferencePoint, 2013.

Rachel Stuckey, *Energy from Living Things: Biomass Energy.* New York: Crabtree Publishing Company, 2016.

WEBSITES

Bureau of Labor Statistics: Careers in Biofuels
https://www.bls.gov/green/biofuels/biofuels.htm

On the website of the Bureau of Labor Statistics, the government agency that studies the nation's workforce, learn more about biofuels and the many careers that support this industry.

Department of Energy: Renewable Energy
https://energy.gov/science-innovation/energy-sources/renewable-energy

The website of the Department of Energy, the US agency that promotes innovative energy policies, features information about all kinds of renewable energy sources, including biomass energy.

National Renewable Energy Laboratory
https://www.nrel.gov/workingwithus/re-biomass.html

On the website of the National Renewable Energy Laboratory, learn about biomass energy and the latest research studies being conducted on biomass and other renewable energy sources.

US Energy Information Administration
https://www.eia.gov/energyexplained/?page=biomass_home

The US Energy Information Administration collects and analyzes data about energy. The website includes statistics, reports, maps, charts, and forecasts about energy usage, industries, and fuels.

cover: nostal6ie/Shutterstock Images

4: MPI/Archive Photos/Getty Images

5: Kodda/Shutterstock Images

8: Quality Stock Arts/Shutterstock Images

15: Jacob Lund/Shutterstock Images

21: Belish/Shutterstock Images

26: Rudmer Zwerver/Shutterstock Images

35: Zvonimir Atletic/Shutterstock Images

37: Danny E Hooks/Shutterstock Images

48: Sponner/Shutterstock Images

52: Rich Carey/Shutterstock Images

62: Warren Gretz/NREL/DOE

67: Science Source

ABOUT THE AUTHOR

Cecilia Pinto McCarthy has written several nonfiction books. When she is not writing, she teaches ecology classes at a nature sanctuary. She lives with her family north of Boston, Massachusetts.